22.

RETURNS

FOR SALE
WITHDRAWN
FROM STOCK

D0493150

Hockey

Rita Storey

W
FRANKLIN WATTS
LONDON • SYDNEY

First published in 2010 by
Franklin Watts
338 Euston Road
London NW1 3BH

Franklin Watts Australia
Level 17/207 Kent Street
Sydney NSW 2000

Copyright © Franklin Watts 2010
Series editor: Julia Bird
Art director: Jonathan Hair

Series designed and created for Franklin Watts by Storeybooks.
Designer: Rita Storey
Editor: Nicola Barber
Photography: Tudor Photography, Banbury (unless otherwise stated)

Picture credits
© MOHSIN RAZA/Reuters/Corbis p9 © Wang Changshan/Xinhua Press/Corbis p27;
Bradley Kanaris/Getty Images p26; i-stock pp22 and 26; Shutterstock pp24.

Thanks to Peter Jackson, Aathavan Lingeswaran, Sarah Haycroft, Patrick Smith and
Georgia Rawlinson for their participation in this book.

A CIP catalogue record for this book is available from the British Library.

Dewey classification: 796.3'55
ISBN: 978 0 7496 9539 2

Printed in China

Franklin Watts is a division of Hachette
Children's Books, an Hachette UK company.
www.hachette.co.uk.

Words in **bold** are in the glossary on page 30.

Contents

Meet the players

Hockey, sometimes known as field hockey to avoid confusion with ice hockey, is a fast and exciting outdoor sport played by two teams of 11 players. The object of the game is to score as many goals as possible – and to stop the opposing team from scoring. There are some similarities between the rules of hockey and football, but in hockey the players use sticks instead of their feet to play the ball.

Most people play hockey at school, or for a local club. They play for enjoyment and to keep fit. Some talented players go on to represent their club, their county and even their country.

In this book you will meet five players who are aiming to play hockey at the highest level. They will share their experiences with you of the training and dedication it takes to make that happen. All the players are currently in the England Under 18 (U18) **squad**.

Early hockey
The first club to play hockey was the Blackheath Football and Hockey Club, in 1861. The game was very different from the modern game played today – in fact it was closer to **rugby football***. It was played with a rubber cube instead of a ball. In 1871 the Teddington Hockey Club developed a version of the game that was much closer to modern hockey – and they replaced the cube with a ball.*

Aathavan Lingeswaran
I am 17 years old and I am a forward or midfield player.

I started playing hockey at school. I have played for the school first team for the past two years.

I played for Surrey County from age 13 to 17, and for the U14s and U15s for South West England. I also played for the England U16s.

My hobbies are playing cricket, watching films and listening to music.

Squad: Wessex Leopards
Club: Holcombe Hockey Club

Georgia Rawlinson
I am 17 years old and I play as a **midfielder** *or* **forward***. I first played hockey for my school, then I went on to play for Gloucestershire.*

As well as hockey, I also enjoy playing tennis, seeing friends, watching films and listening to music.

Squad: Wessex Leopards
Club: Cannock Hockey Club

Sarah Haycroft
I am 18 years old and I play midfield or forward (centre half or inside forward).

I first started playing hockey for my school when I was ten years old. I joined Surbiton Hockey Club when I was 12 and also represented my county (Surrey). More recently I have been picked for the England U21s.

As well as hockey, I also enjoy skiing and shopping.

Squad: Wessex Leopards
Club: Surbiton Hockey Club

Patrick Smith
I am 18 years old and I play in the position of goalkeeper.
I began playing hockey at primary school when I was nine and went on to join Saffron Walden Hockey Club when I was ten. I continued to play for my club up to senior level. I now play with the England U18s.

As well as hockey, I enjoy playing the piano, cricket, table tennis, pool and tennis, and going out with my mates.

Squad: Mercia Lynx
Club: Southgate Hockey Club

Peter Jackson
*I am 18 years old and play halfback (midfield) and fullback (**defender**).*

I played hockey for my school from Year 8. I played county hockey for Cheshire from the age of 13, winning the U15 County Championships when I was 14, and captaining the side a year later when we were runners-up. I have also been in the U17 and U21 county sides, as well as the North West U15s and U17s. I now play for the England U18 team.

My hobbies and interests are keeping fit by going to the gym and running, as well as most sports. I also enjoy listening to music and being with friends.

Squad: Pennine Pumas
Club: Brooklands MUHC

Starting out

Hockey is one of the most popular team sports in the world. It is played in more than 100 countries worldwide.

Mini hockey

For very young players, there is a seven-a-side version of hockey called mini hockey. It is played for a shorter time and on a smaller pitch than normal hockey.

School hockey

Hockey is a popular team sport in many schools. Those who enjoy it, and are good at it, play for school teams and take part in inter-school competitions such as the National Schools Championships. Hockey is also one of the sports played at the National School Games. This annual four-day championship features ten sports and is designed to have the feel of a major event such as the Olympic Games.

I started playing hockey on a summer sports camp at my primary school at the age of nine. I was put in goal as I had never played before. I really enjoyed it and wasn't bad either. I wasn't old enough to play in goal for the school team so I started as an **outfield player***, but this only lasted a year and from then on I have been playing in between the posts!*

Most young people have their first experience of playing hockey at school.

I first played hockey at school during a PE lesson while I had a broken ankle – just messing around with a stick. I enjoyed it and then went to some training sessions to take part in the Cheshire Youth Games.

When I was 14 I had to make a choice at school between hockey, football and rugby. Hockey was the sport I enjoyed the most, so I carried on with it. Because it was the only sport I was playing I found it easier to focus on.

*I played football and cricket at junior school and represented Surrey County at cricket from age 11 to 14. I only started playing hockey at secondary school because it was **compulsory**!*

Hockey clubs

There are nearly 1,000 hockey clubs in England alone. Hockey clubs run league hockey, which is played at weekends. There are regional and county leagues with the top men's and women's clubs playing nationally in the English Hockey League. Hockey clubs usually have youth sections that young players can join.

Indoor hockey

There is a six-a-side version of hockey that is played indoors. It is a fast and very physical version of field hockey. The rules are similar, but there are barriers for the ball to bounce off instead of side-lines. The National Indoor Hockey Championships are held every year for both junior and senior men and women. The winners go on to compete in the EuroHockey Indoor Nations Challenge and the Indoor World Cup.

I first started playing hockey at school when I was ten.

I enjoyed hockey because it is a fast game that's fun, and I was good at it. I am a very competitive person – I loved the competition!

My first coach, Adele Brown, has encouraged me right from the start of my hockey career.

I started off having one hockey lesson at school and really enjoyed it, so I joined the local club and was selected from there to play for my county.

I like the idea of being in a team, meeting different people, and the satisfaction when you improve and are successful.

Taking it further

For hockey players who show real talent, there are schemes available that give them financial support and allow them access to the best training facilities.

National Age Group Squads

Some countries, including England, select hockey players to represent the country at U16, U18 and U21 levels. In order to be selected, players have to attend Junior Development Centres, Junior Academy Centres, Junior Regional Performance Centres and High Performance Assessment Camps, as well as continuing to play for their club or school.

Training as a team

To play hockey at a high level means learning to fit quickly into a team of players. In England, players who are selected to join the High Performance Assessment Camps play for one of four squads: the Saxon Tigers, the Pennine Pumas, the Wessex Leopards or the Mercia Lynx.

Selection for one of these four squads is a real honour. Players in the squads take part in the England Hockey Futures Cup, a competition for players in the U16 and U18 age groups.

At the Futures Cup, the National Age Group Squads are selected. These squads represent England in international competitions. They take part in one of the Four Nations Invitational Tournaments at Easter (with Germany, Spain and

Hockey in Scotland and Wales

The Scottish Hockey Union and the Welsh Hockey Union are the national governing bodies for field hockey in Scotland and Wales. They both run development programmes through clubs, schools and universities. These programmes supply the training needs of players from grassroots right through to international level.

Coach's notes: developing potential

To allow a player to develop his or her full potential, we need to recognise talent early. Once we have spotted a good player then the systems are in place to allow him or her to progress. How far a player gets is as much to do with commitment as it is with talent.

Go for gold

The ultimate prize for a hockey player is a gold medal at the Olympic Games, held every four years. A Great Britain (GB) team competes in the Olympics. The players in the GB team are selected from England, Scotland, Wales and Northern Ireland.

South African player Andrew Cronje (right) clears an attack by Japan's Koji Kayukawa during a match in the Asian Four Nations Junior Hockey Tournament.

I was captain of the team that won the Four Nations Tournament in 2009. Finishing ahead of big hockey nations such as Spain, Germany and the Netherlands was a brilliant success.

the Netherlands) and the **biennial** Home Nations Tournament in July (with Scotland, Wales and Ireland).

National Performance Centres

England Hockey have set up six National Performance Centres (NPCs) in England. These centres have facilities where selected players aged between 18 and 23 years can access top-quality coaching, strength and **conditioning** training, **physiotherapy** and lifestyle support.

One of the England Hockey National Performance Centres is based at Birmingham University where I am reading maths. At this NPC I am provided with top-quality coaching. I also have a training programme that will guide me in the right direction to achieve the goals I have set.

Good coaching is vital to the ongoing development of a hockey player's career. Coaches work closely with the players on all aspects of their game, as well as their fitness and personal development.

Recognising potential

One important job for a coach at school or club level is to recognise potential in young players. Encouraging young people, as well as teaching them good basic skills, is invaluable for those who want to take the game further.

Di Reed, from Newport Free Grammar Secondary School, coaches all the young goalkeepers in my local area. She gave me the best possible start when I began playing, encouraging me to join Saffron Walden Hockey Club at the age of ten. She coached me on all the basics and has always been there if I needed a push in the right direction or some advice on the phone. One day I hope to thank her by achieving gold at an Olympic Games.

Sarah practises under the watchful eye of one of her coaches.

My main coach is very level-headed, controlled and calm, but she is also very good at motivating the team and getting the best out of the group.

She is analytical, and is constantly reviewing and assessing my performance in order to help me improve. She also gives me **drills** *or exercises that are helpful if I need to improve a certain part of my game.*

After matches she uses video footage to analyse the play.

We also use **possession statistics** *(see page 11) to analyse performance.*

Watching video playbacks of matches is a good way of assessing how a player's skills and tactics can be improved.

Looking ahead

Players who have been recognised as having the talent and dedication needed to progress to a high level will often have more than one coach. Some coaches may be specialists in areas such as strength and fitness. Other coaches will be the team coaches for their club, county or country. The coaches are responsible for identifying the long-, medium- and short-term **objectives** for each player.

Performance analysis

Coaches use a variety of different ways to analyse the performance of a player. Playing back videos of matches can help to show up any weaknesses. Possession statistics are used to analyse the number of times the ball is lost to the opponents (**turnovers**), and how many times members of the team manage to penetrate the opponents' line of defence.

Coach's notes: believing

Believing that you can do something is the first step on the road to being able to achieve it. It is up to the coach to encourage each individual player to believe in his or her own ability. Only then can players do the best for themselves, for their team and for their fellow players.

In training

Competitive hockey players need to be strong and physically fit to perform at their best and avoid getting injured. This means regular training on the pitch, in the gym and at home.

Building stamina

There are two halves in a hockey game, each one lasting 35 minutes. The players run the length and width of the pitch at speed many times during a game. To do this, and play effectively, they need a very high level of **stamina** and physical fitness.

Types of exercises

Cardiovascular These exercises are designed to increase the heart rate and strengthen the heart

I do strength, flexibility and fitness training, but not always in the gym. Normally I do strength and flexibility training at home, and fitness training out on the pitch.

I have a strength and conditioning coach, which I fund myself. She sets me a programme to make sure I'm in peak condition for tournaments. The programme includes strength and power exercises, as well as flexibility at the end of sessions.

Georgia and Sarah use the cross-trainers in the gym. These machines simulate walking or running and help to build stamina and core stability.

I do strength, flexibility training and fitness training once a week in the gym. I do simple exercises at home every day.

This core stability exercise, called 'the plank', is one that can easily be done at home.

Training with weights helps to build muscles in the legs that give explosive power for sprinting.

and lungs. This means that players can exercise more intensively without getting out of breath. It also increases their tolerance to **lactic acid** and **adrenalin**. These chemicals build up in the bloodstream and cause pain in the muscles after hard exercise.

Core stability Exercises that target core stability strengthen the trunk of the body, which is made up of more than 30 separate muscles across the back, stomach and hips. This type of exercise gives an athlete a solid foundation of fitness and helps to prevent injury.

Flexibility Stretching exercises help the players to reach and bend to the maximum without injuring themselves.

Power Exercises that strengthen muscle help players to introduce an explosive burst of speed when they need it.

Training on the pitch allows players to practise the skills they will need to use in a match. The hockey season in the United Kingdom lasts from September until May. However, many players train nearly all year round, as the summer is often used for extra workshops and training camps. Nearly all hockey pitches are now made of an artificial playing surface called astroturf.

Warming up and cooling down

Before a training session the players do a series of stretches as they move around, called **dynamic stretches**. These stretches and drills warm up the muscles and prepare the players to perform at their maximum.

Quick thinking

Hockey players need to be very alert to outwit their opponents. To avoid a tackle or an

Georgia is warming up with some dynamic stretches.

Training gives you a sense of responsibility – if you don't do the work you will fall behind. This also relates to other aspects of life, including school studies. Training also promotes a good team spirit.

Jogging round the pitch helps the players to warm up before training.

interception (see page 17) they practise a variety of ways of confusing attackers and keeping **possession** of the ball. An example is a move called the 'dummy and drag'. The player in possession of the ball begins to run one way then, just as his or her opponent reaches for the ball, changes direction and drags it the opposite way out of reach.

These skills are practised in drills, as well as in games played with just a few players on each side. Practice games allow the players to try out their skills in a match situation.

Cool down

At the end of a session, players do another series of stretches to cool down. These stretches are held for a longer time and done while the player is still (**static stretches**). Static stretches allow the muscles to relax and prevent them from stiffening up and causing **cramp**.

I train five days a week. The duration varies depending on what I am doing. For example, a session can be an hour-long core skill session, or a two-hour club training session. Training always starts with a warm up and ends with a cool down.

Coach's notes: training

Training is the key to winning. Hockey players need strength, speed and the ability to think and act in a split second if they are to have any chance of winning. Having the right mental attitude often comes from putting in the training – that way you know you are not fooling yourself.

I train three days a week: 25 minutes warm up, two hours training, cool down for 20 minutes.

Core skills

Some skills are specific to a player's position. Other skills, called core skills, **are common to every position and players must practise them regularly. In hockey the core skills are passing and receiving, tackling and running with the ball. These skills are practised over and over again.**

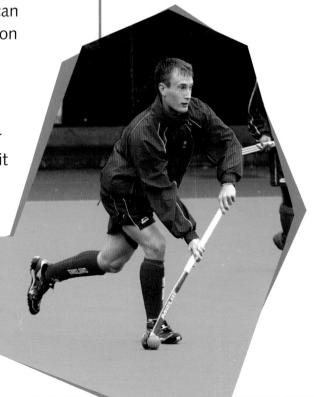

Running with the ball is normally improved by drills that change direction, and specific core skills such as V-drags (see below).

Passing

Part of the skill of accurate passing is being aware of exactly what is happening around you. To make a perfect pass, it is necessary to judge the speed and direction of the team mate you intend to pass to. The ball should be positioned so that it can be controlled easily by your team mate as he or she receives it. Passing the ball moves it forward faster than running with it.

Receiving

Once a ball has been passed to you, it is vital that you get control of it straight away. At this point it can either be passed to another player in a better position to move it forward, or you may choose to move it forward yourself.

Peter runs with the ball. He is keeping the ball close to his stick and is watching what is happening around him.

Running with the ball

Moving the ball is done either by running with it or by tapping the ball from side to side while moving it forwards. This is called **dribbling**. Various drills are used in training to improve ball control while running with the ball. In the V-drag drill a 'V' shape is set up on the ground with cones or markers. The player plays the ball down the left of the V, drags it back to the middle, then moves it down the right of the V and accelerates forward.

Tackling and intercepting

If a player on the opposing team is in possession of the ball you may be in a position to tackle and try to take the ball away from him or her. This is a tricky manoeuvre because if you hit either your opponent's stick or body it is a **foul**. It is necessary to have precise timing and to aim directly for the ball. The point where a ball is being passed from one player to another is a perfect moment to intercept and take control. To make an interception, the attacking player needs to be thinking one step ahead of his or her opponent.

Three cards

Players are shown coloured cards if they commit a foul in a hockey match. A green card is a warning given for a minor foul. A yellow card is shown for a more serious foul and the player must leave the pitch for five minutes. A red card is shown for serious or dangerous fouls and the player must leave the pitch for the rest of the game.

Simple passing and receiving drills are useful, as the best way to improve your core skills is to do many repetitions of a skill. Everyone practises the V-drag drill as this improves control while running with the ball, which is vital whatever position you play in.

Sarah's team mates watch her practising a V-drag drill (see page 16). This drill is used to improve control while running with the ball.

The goalkeeper

The skills and training required to be a good goalkeeper are very different from those needed by the rest of the players in a hockey team. The job of the goalkeeper is to keep the ball out of the net. He or she can do this by using any part of the body, as well as the stick.

Protective kit

A hockey ball can travel towards the goal at a frightening 120 kilometres an hour. To protect the goalkeeper from the force of the ball, he or she wears a range of protective clothing. This includes a helmet and face mask, padded gloves, a protective jacket for the upper body, padded leg guards and shoe covers called kickers. Lightweight foam products are not heavy, but they are bulky to wear, and goalkeepers must still be agile and flexible.

Types of save

Low balls are stopped with the feet and kicked or hit clear of the goal. High balls are blocked with the stick

Tactics play a big part in my game. As a keeper, I need to read the game constantly and organise my defence accordingly. Having an understanding of the tactics of the game helps massively.

*My favourite parts of training are shooting drills and **penalty corners** (see pages 20–21), as I am in the thick of the action. I am not so keen on training matches. In the middle of winter it can get a little cold standing in the D (the striking circle – see page 30) waiting for the forwards to attack the goal!*

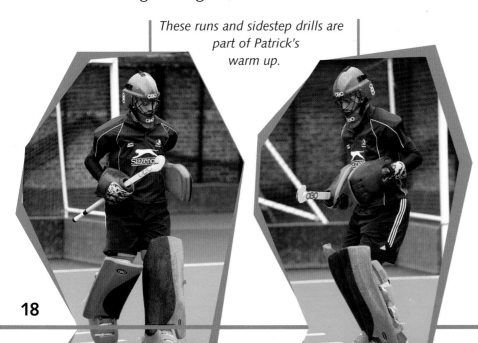

These runs and sidestep drills are part of Patrick's warm up.

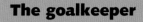

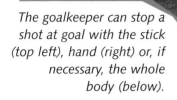

The goalkeeper can stop a shot at goal with the stick (top left), hand (right) or, if necessary, the whole body (below).

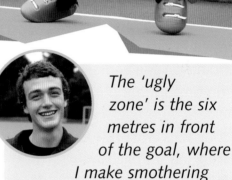

or the hands. A keeper can also make a diving save to block the goal with his or her body and stick. This is called a '**log**'.

Reactions

Goalkeepers must have lightning reactions. Watching the game closely helps them to anticipate the direction from which a shot might be coming. Even though the goalkeeper is not running around the pitch as much as the rest of the players, core fitness is still essential. A goalkeeper must stretch and bend to make saves and can easily get injured if not fully fit.

Penalties

A **penalty** stroke is given when a dangerous foul or other serious offence happens in the striking circle (see page 30). The penalty shot is taken from a spot 6.4 metres directly in front of the goal. The goalkeeper must stand with his or her heels on the goal-line until the ball is played. When the umpire blows the whistle, the striker may take one step and push or flick the ball at the goal.

The 'ugly zone' is the six metres in front of the goal, where I make smothering saves and reaction saves. It is from this area, and from penalty corners, that most goals are scored.

The actual time on the pitch during which I am directly involved is significantly less than the outfield players. However, when I am involved everything I do is massively pressured, because if I make a mistake it usually results in a goal.

The team

There are 11 players in a hockey team, including the goalkeeper. Apart from the goalkeeper there are no set positions for the rest of the players. They are usually split into forwards, midfielders and defenders.

Different formations

Much the same as in a football game, the defenders, midfielders and forwards can be played in different formations depending on the captain's tactics.

A common formation is five forwards, three midfielders, two backs and a goalkeeper (5–3–2), as is four forwards, three midfielders, three fullbacks and a goalkeeper (4–3–3).

Forwards

Positions – left wing, right wing, left inside forward, right inside forward, and centre forward

The forwards in a hockey team are the main goal scorers. They spend most of their time between the midfield and the opponent's goal.

Scoring goals is the object of hockey so the goal-scoring skills of the forwards can be match winners. Forwards spend a considerable amount of their training working on shooting practice and taking penalties (see page 19) and penalty corners.

A penalty corner is given to the opposing team if a player deliberately plays the ball over the back-line.

(see page 19)

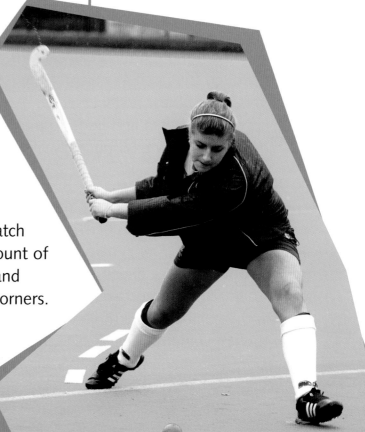

Forwards need to be able to spot gaps in the opponent's defence, and have the skills to be able to score from them.

Coach's notes: teamwork

There are no free rides in a hockey team. Having great goal-scorers is a real asset, but without the back-up of the rest of the team they won't get the opportunity to use their skills. A goal may be put in the net by one player, but to get it there is a team effort.

The defending players surge forward as soon as a penalty corner shot is taken.

When a penalty corner is being taken, up to five players from the defending team (including the goalkeeper) must stand behind the back-line (see page 30). The rest of the team have to move back behind the halfway-line. The player taking the penalty hits the ball from the back-line to a point outside the circle. As soon as the ball moves, the defenders can leave the lines and try to stop the opposition's strikers scoring a goal. A lot of goals are scored from penalty corners, so the players practise their tactics over and over again.

Midfielders

Positions – left half, right half and centre half
Midfield players both defend and attack. They are the link between the forwards and the backs. They must have plenty of stamina to get into position wherever they are needed.

Defenders

Positions – left fullback, right fullback and goalkeeper
The job of the backs is to defend against the forwards on the opposing team. The backs also try to clear the ball when it gets close to the goal.

In a training session, we do 20 minutes of penalty corner attack and penalty corner defence. We jog the length of the pitch in between.
We also do a drill called a 'three-man weave'. In this drill, the ball is passed while on the move between three players. It improves the core skill of passing and receiving the ball.

Lifestyle

Hockey players who are training at a high level have very little time to themselves. Evenings are regularly spent training, and matches take up weekends. This means that seeing friends and socialising can be difficult to fit in. Keeping up with school work can require a lot of discipline.

Eating to be fit

All athletes need a good, balanced diet to stay heathy and perform well. They do not usually restrict the amount of food they eat, but they must ensure that it is the right sort of food. Fruit and vegetables are essential for providing the **nutrients** and **minerals** needed. Along with these, a high-**carbohydrate**, high-**protein** and low-fat diet is necessary to give the body the energy to train well each day. Most hockey players eat their share of goodies such as chocolate, but limit them to occasional 'treats'.

I eat a balanced diet – lots of carbohydrates (rice, pasta) and a sufficient intake of proteins from chicken, fish and lentils. I regularly eat salads and vegetables. I also drink two cups of milk every day. I used to eat a lot of fruit but I'm a bit fussy now (typical teenager!).

I have no restrictions – I allow myself lots of treats. As I am training and playing a lot, whatever I eat is used up. My weight is not a problem.

A healthy diet does not have to be boring. This colourful chicken pasta salad is full of all the right ingredients.

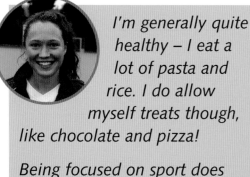

I'm generally quite healthy – I eat a lot of pasta and rice. I do allow myself treats though, like chocolate and pizza!

Being focused on sport does mean that you miss out on parties and spending time with friends.

Peter takes a drink to rehydrate his body after an exhausting training session.

Water

Drinking the right amount of water is important for keeping your body healthy. Being **dehydrated** can have a negative impact on an athlete's performance.

Education

All the hockey players in this book are combining their hockey training with their education. Balancing homework and exams with playing sport at a high level can be tricky. However, athletes have to be very disciplined to train and perform well, so it is not altogether surprising that they can be disciplined in other areas of their life too.

I train two days a week at school and play at least one match for school every Saturday. Then on Sundays I either train or play a match for the county, regionals or nationals. As I have limited time I have to be very organised. I have deadlines to hand over school work, so I do it as soon as it's given and don't wait until the last minute. I catch up on school work during the school holidays.

I have to organise my time well and try to do all my school work as soon as possible so it doesn't all pile up. But overall it isn't that much of a problem, as long as I have a routine.

I have missed out on some social aspects of being a teenager. For example, I missed my school leavers' ball.

I have just finished school at Kingston Grammar and I am going to study at Birmingham University next year.

Matches

All of a hockey player's training is put to the test in a match. Preparation for important matches must be carefully controlled so that young players are at the peak of fitness just at the right time.

Players are involved in lots of different matches throughout the season as they may play for a school team as well as a club, a national age group squad and even their country.

Part of a team

Having other members of the team around you can relieve some of the pressure before and after a match. There is always someone to discuss tactics with, and to talk to about the result.

Before a match

Some players like to do exactly the same things before every important match to bring them luck.

I always eat the same cereal on the day of a match. I like to relax before the match and listen to my iPod.

Motivation

The coach and the captain are the two people who **motivate** the team. The belief that you can win is very important, particularly against a strong team.

Players frequently push themselves to the limit to try to win a match for their country. Here, Korean Lee Nam Yong (right) steals the ball away from the opposing Malaysian players in an AirAsia Men's Asia Cup hockey tournament.

Mentally, I start preparing for a big match one week in advance. However, I don't exercise or train more – I train as I usually do. I like to do things the same way, otherwise I become nervous. I do simple exercises that keep me fit.

I eat loads of pasta, rice and nuts to store carbohydrates in my body.

I don't eat oily or spicy food on the day of the match. I try to have porridge and toast with peanut butter for breakfast, and to drink plenty of fluids.

Specialist motivational coaches are employed to work with **elite** athletes to improve their self-belief.

The result of a hockey game is not certain until the last whistle blows. Staying motivated right to the end of a match may be difficult, particularly if things are not going well. A good captain will be able to keep things calm and focus the players on doing what they have trained so hard to do.

Coach's notes: the captain

A good team captain earns rather than demands the respect of the rest of the players. The captain keeps everyone focused so that they don't panic if they are losing, or allow themselves to relax if they are winning. It is a particular type of person who can do this without letting his or her own performance suffer.

*I think a captain can do a lot to lift the morale of a team and to get everyone working together. The captain must also lead by example – and it's not only words that encourage the team. The captain can set the tone with their own play, intensity and **work rate**.*

Match rules

The International Hockey Federation (FIH) is the global governing body for hockey. It organises international events such as the Hockey World Cup and Women's Hockey World Cup. It also writes the rules for hockey.

S orting hero s

Successful hockey players are an inspiration to those who are training hard to reach the top of their sport.

I would like to play like Helen Richardson.

She's got amazing skills and work rate, and great commitment.

Helen Richardson
England and Great Britain Defender
Date of birth: 23 Nov 1981

2007, 2005 and 1999 EuroHockey Nations Championship: Bronze
2007 and 2002 Champions Challenge: Bronze and Gold
2006 and 2002 Commonwealth Games: Bronze and Silver

Just under 100 caps for England

Helen Richardson (left) of Great Britain challenges Melanie Wells for the ball during the Third Test match between the Australian Hockeyroos and Great Britain at the State Hockey Centre in Brisbane, Australia.

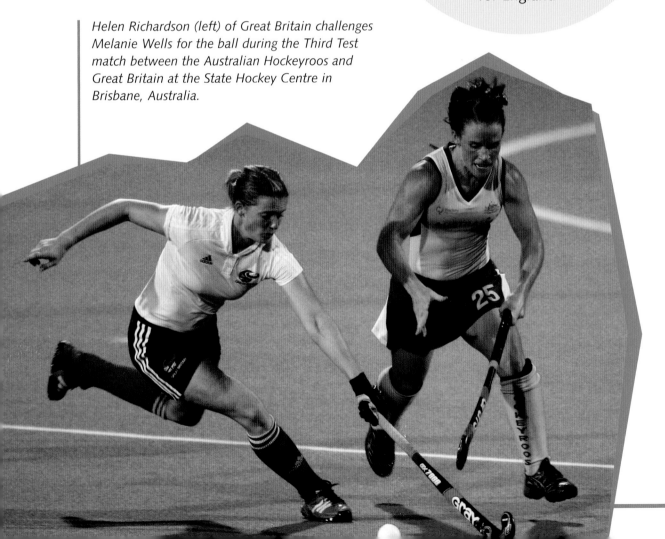

The international hockey player who I aspire to be like is Brett Garrard.

Brett was one of my first coaches, so from a young age I looked up to him. He always wants to help and improve young hockey players, and being the GB men's captain, he could not have achieved more in his own playing career.

He is so calm and controlled on the ball and seems as though he has so much time. He is a great passer of the ball and can hit long to forwards or thread passes through into the midfield.

I really admire Robert van der Horst. He is one of the best defenders in the world. I try to copy his range of passing options – they don't always work, but I'm getting there slowly.

Robert van der Horst (front) of the Netherlands tussles with Marian Schole of Canada for the ball at the 2008 Olympic Games.

Robert van der Horst
The Netherlands
Midfielder/defender
Date of birth: 17 Oct 1984

2007 European Championships: Gold
2007 Champions Trophy: Bronze
2006 Champions Trophy: Gold
2005 European Championships: Silver
2004 and 2005 Champions Trophy: Silver
2005 World Hockey Young Player of the Year

T e next st p

Field hockey is an elite Olympic sport that requires dedication as well as skill and talent. Hockey players may continue to play at a high level into their late twenties and early thirties.

In some countries hockey is a professional sport, but in the UK players rely mainly on sponsorship to help with travel and other costs.

Injuries

Hockey is not a dangerous sport to play, but injuries can occur in all sports. Even though they may not stop a player participating in a sport, they may stop him or her performing at the highest level. Having a back-up plan is always advisable.

When their playing days are at an end, some players remain in the sport as professional coaches, passing on their expertise to another generation of players, or in more administrative roles. Others may continue to be involved at club level simply for enjoyment while pursuing another career.

Patrick, Peter, Aathavan, Sarah and Georgia are all keeping their options open by combining their academic studies with their careers in hockey.

My ultimate ambition is to captain Great Britain in an Olympic Games and win gold.

I am working for a degree in mathematics, so if I have an injury that ends my hockey career I do have a contingency plan in place. Outside hockey, I would probably pursue a career in law. I would certainly like to be involved in hockey if I couldn't play any more, for example taking up a coaching role.

Ultimately my goal is to be selected to go to the Olympics. My next target is to be selected for the U21 squad. In five years' time, if all goes well, I will hopefully be playing for the senior team.

My goal is to play for the England U21s and then the England seniors.

To do that I'm going to have to work hard!

My next target is to get into the England U21 team. My ultimate ambition is to play for England seniors.

In five years' time I want to be playing at the highest standard I can, and possibly have the experience of playing abroad.

I was part of the England U18 team that won the gold cup in the 2009 Four Nations Tournament in Spain.

When we held the cup I felt that all our efforts were worthwhile. It was a pleasure to see our coaches and parents smiling and clapping for our victory.

International competitions

For all sportsmen and women there is something very special about representing your country in international competitions. In hockey, the main international events are the Olympic Games, the hockey World Cup, the Commonwealth Games, the Champions Challenge and the Champions Trophy. All these players aspire to perform at that level. We wish them all well.

Aathavan, Peter, Patrick, Sarah and Georgia know they have a lot of hard work in front of them to achieve their ambitions as hockey players.

Glossary

adrenalin A hormone that is released into the bloodstream in response to physical or mental stress. It stimulates the body to perform at its maximum level.

astroturf A type of artificial playing surface used for sports pitches.

biennial Describes something that happens every two years.

carbohydrate A group of foods that includes sugars and starches.

cardiovascular The system that carries blood to and from all parts of the body.

compulsory Something that has to be done.

conditioning Exercise that improves physical fitness.

core skills In hockey, skills that are common to every position in the team.

core stability The strength of the muscles in the trunk of the body. Exercise that targets the core gives an athlete a solid foundation of fitness and helps to prevent injury.

cramp A sudden, sometimes painful, contraction of a muscle.

defenders In hockey, anyone on the team not in possession of the ball.

dehydrated Suffering from a lack of water.

dribbling In hockey, moving the ball forward by tapping it from side to side with the stick.

drill An exercise practised again and again to perfect a skill.

dynamic stretch A stretching exercise done whilst on the move.

elite A group of people who are at the top level in their sport.

flexibility the ability to bend easily

forwards In hockey, the main goal scorers who spend most of their time between the midfield and the opponent's goal.

foul Breaking a rule in a sport or game.

lactic acid A substance produced in the muscles during exercise. Too much lactic acid can cause cramping pains.

log In hockey, a diving save that blocks the goal with the goalkeeper's body and stick.

midfielders Players that both defend and attack. They are the link between the forwards and the backs.

minerals Elements in food such as calcium, iron, magnesium, potassium and sodium. They are essential for our bodies to function correctly.

motivation The reason why a person wants to achieve something.

nutrients The substances in food that are used by the body to grow and stay healthy.

objective Something that a person works to achieve.

outfield player Refers to all of the members of a hockey team with the exception of the goalkeeper.

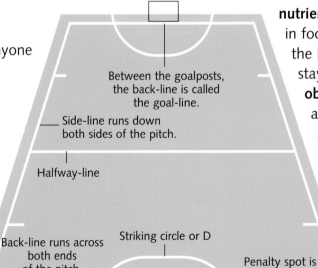

Between the goalposts, the back-line is called the goal-line.

Side-line runs down both sides of the pitch.

Halfway-line

Back-line runs across both ends of the pitch.

Striking circle or D

Penalty spot is 6.4m from the goal-line.

A field hockey pitch

penalty A disadvantage imposed on a competitor for breaking a rule.

penalty corner In hockey, a free hit from the end-line given to the opposing team if a player deliberately plays the ball over the back-line.

physiotherapy The treatment of injuries with exercise.

possession Having the ball.

possession statistics Analysis that shows the number of times the ball is lost to the other team, and how many times team members break through the opponents' line of defence.

power mechanical or physical energy.

protein A group of foods that includes meat, fish and cheese.

rugby football The sport usually referred to as rugby (as opposed to rugby league).

squad A group of players from which a team is selected.

stamina The ability to exercise intensely for a long period of time.

static stretch A stretching exercise done whilst remaining in one place.

turnover When the ball is lost to the opponents.

work rate The percentage of someone's full physical potential that is being used by that person.

Find out more

Websites

http://www.englandhockey.co.uk
The official site for hockey in England. A lot of general information as well as video highlights and up-to-date results. There is also information about Great Britain Hockey.

http://www.scottish-hockey.org.uk
The official site for hockey in Scotland. News and information about all aspects of Scottish hockey, including up-to-date results.

http://www.welsh-hockey.co.uk
The official site for hockey in Wales. It has information on Welsh hockey at every level from school and club hockey to international competitions.

http://www.sportplan.com/drills/Hockey/features/index.jsp
Watch videos of a range of warm up exercises as well as drills, exercises and masterclasses to improve your hockey technique.

Books

Know Your Sport: Hockey (Franklin Watts, 2008)
A guide to field hockey, with step-by-step photographs and explanations of some of the shots as well as profiles and statistics giving information about some of the world's greatest players.

Note to parents and teachers: every effort has been made by the Publishers to ensure that these websites are suitable for children, that they are of the highest educational value, and that they contain no inappropriate or offensive material. However, because of the nature of the Internet, it is impossible to guarantee that the contents of these sites will not be altered. We strongly advise that Internet access is supervised by a responsible adult.

Index